THE SERMONS OF JEAN HARLOW

&

THE CURSES OF BILLY THE KID

Michael McClure

⚜

The Sermons of

Jean Harlow

& the Curses of

Billy the Kid

⚜

1968
FOUR SEASONS FOUNDATION
with
DAVE HASELWOOD BOOKS
S. F.

Distributed by City Lights Books
1562 Grant Ave., San Francisco 94111

Library of Congress Catalog Card Number: 67-31397

THE SERMONS OF JEAN HARLOW

THE CURSES OF BILLY THE KID

JEAN HARLOW

OH GOD, HOW SUPERB IT IS, TO BE INFINITELY BEAUTIFUL!
OH GOD, AMONG THE PLUMES AND RAINBOWS
floating in air! I LOVE IT!
And the dark woods! — My arms among them!
THE GLIMMER OF THE PLANKS OF THE VEIL
making all this! Do you see it!? It is sheer,
REALLY ALL SHEER!
Oh, thank God, I am breathing
and I lift my chin in the air!
I feel my breasts move
and the muscles in them
make circles
and the blood warms the back of my neck
and my slender arms bulge!
My blonde hair falls in my face
and my mouth breathes in
almost making a smile. . .
And I reach one finger
into the air
and press it — it giggles at me
my surprise to see
and I fall
in the hall
of my senses. Touching the hole
to love. AHH! OH! OH!
OOOOOOOHHHHHHH

THE KID

THANK GOD I AM HERE! I WILL KILL ALL THOSE
WHO OFFEND ME
THEN I'LL STEP THROUGH THE RAINBOW
at the top of the Cliff! I'll walk
on them, with my plumed boots in their faces
I shall run over their chests
and dance naked on their children
with the moon behind me making a sil-
houette! GOD DAMN THESE FUCKING BASTARDS
WHO KILL!!
I'll destroy each
of them! AND THEN I'LL TORTURE
THEIR SOULS
in Hell!!!
TANK
KNIFE
CRASHER!!
Rose
WAVE
drip
breath
sweet
INFERNO!

JEAN HARLOW

OH GOD I WANT TO TELL YOU I LOVE YOU,
WITH OR WITHOUT THE PAINT ON MY LIPS.
Oh God, I love you as the slips
of flowers blossoming in May
or the chrome sportscar
exploding in play !
IT IS ALL REAL—I THINK,
as an ankle in satin
of blue or of cream
in the dream-stream where thoughts beam !
And I step from the wreck with a grin
one speck of oil on my shin
and roll my eyes upward
to
YOU. . .
Not even the strap on my slip
is broken.

And the sky is turquoise melting into blue !
AND THE SKY IS TURQUOISE MELTING INTO BLUE.

THE KID

IT IS ALL A GRAY HELL! THE BLUES BECOME GRAY!
Only a dark brown or a black is worth seeing.
The elves and the fairies are flayed!
Man and God are to blame
for the cruelty and thieving
seething in the kettle!
I've torn the wings off my skull,
but I'll raise
myself in the blaze
by my eyeballs. With my
arms crossed behind my back
grasping my toes in the flack
of the bombs exploding,
while the splashed flames daze
themselves on human meat!
I
SHALL RAISE
MYSELF WITH MY FACE
A YELLOW MASK OF FURY!!!

JEAN HARLOW

THE SKY IS TURQUOISE MELTING TO BLUE,
the sky is turquoise melting to blue
and I love you true
OH GOD!
Oh God in my shape
sweet as a grape
covered with silk and with lace.
I see your white face
loaded with grace
floating in my oval mirror.
The ivory handle loves my hand
the scent of flowers fills the room
where I stand,
while I float ten feet in the air.
Oh, I am true, true, true,
to me and to you and to the fantasy
of my calves. The sunlight burns my skin
but I grow plump in your grace
sailing in the space
where you make me of my dream.
OH.
AHHH
OOOOOOOOOH,
a rhinestone kiss for you . . .
A beaded bag . . .
A satin slipper . . .
And I shall be true to a thousand loves
like mascara melting on skin.

THE KID

WE COIL OUR SKINS IN SMOKE – AS TWISTED AS A FILTHY JOKE.
One lost in the other, turned inside out
upon a spit we make
for each other!
And I stand free
with utter contempt I pee
upon my heap of gold
like a Cherub in a Dionysian Park.
YEAH, it is dark,
owls and bats play with the salamandrine
shark, rotting in their fetish slime
and steal shit from one another.
My brain is a floating feather
in a blast of sun.
I can see ten billion years to anywhere
AND ITS ALL A SHAME!
I'll take one crime and compound it
to a hero's deed
upon a blueblack bridge
OF ICE
and cool my shotgun with a slice
of sheriff's life! HO HUMM!
That's not real!
THAT'S NOT REAL! There's a coil
of sable wire with thorns
that blows this shit to Hell!
And pictures change shape upon a sandy floor!
Oh Yeah!
Crack!

JEAN HARLOW

Turn on and sing my happy song,
Oh God,
and I'll be you !
The way is not long
and I am strong

as an Easter *April* wrapped in red,
the skies are alive or dead,
no difference when you are there, if you are—
IT DOES NOT MATTER
I dance in your glance with toes like fur
I furl myself in air with platinum hair
that drifts in the glare of You
becoming Me. And I see
my dress drop to the floor
upon the beaming knitted rug.
I thank me for my arms, and thank you
for your charms, and me
for my lacquered nails with moons
that wax and wane,
and I know that sane
or insane
DOES NOT MATTER
with taxi driver
or with Duke. Turn on
and sing my happy song
AND I'LL BE YOU . . .

THE KID

LIKE NEW OLD JAZZ COMING THROUGH THE WALLS!
The sound of sickening piano
where owl eyed feathers
TURN TO FLAME
and burn like heather
on an earth turned Gates of Hell destroyed by shame!
The pleasure mongers feel
themselves and peel
their grape.
THE SHIT OF DEATH'S AN ORANGE WALL
that changes shape and crackles!!
DISEMBODIED VOICES FLOAT IN AIR!
and
I DON'T CARE A HAIR.
The cougar and the spider float in their garbage boat
upon the waves of lead.
GOD DAMN YOU! DIE! BE DEAD!
With a buckshot blast
accompanying the last words of Man!
The human tiger wears a lambkin's skin
AND SCREAMS
his dreams
into
a hair-lined
PIT!

I'll make it *new*!

HARLOW & THE KID

Rise up ! Rise up ! The voicelet cries,
the days are a bracelet in your eyes
of filligree and silvered gold
the nights shall never paralyze

※

The Pain that withers in the fold
and bags of flesh and skin that shies
where Babe-in-Youth once laughed and rolled
beneath a light of leather skies

※

The softness of my flesh that swings
before a mild curtain of strings
of colored glass that blows and gleams
like varnished wood beheld by wings

※

And faces drip upon the beams
like torturesques of sagging meat
and silhouettes in crushing streams
break up, and tug and pull the sheet

Where men are halves, dust does not float

※

OH DRUNKEN
Drunken
DRUNKEN
Drunken
DRUNKEN
Drunken
DRUNKEN
Drunken
DRUNKEN
Drunken
HELL OF JOY where we swirl
and furl
THE CYCLONES OF LOVERS
in a dream, in a swarm, where it's warm,
above the soft and polished machines like bees
becoming angels sipping on a neon pelt.
Like a hideous charm exploded
to the size of a world
but touching cheeks again
and human above the wooden flames!
BUT HERE IS MY HAND — I AM REAL AGAIN.
Here is my breast I am real again,
the nipple is a rose...

HERE IS MY THORN, MY HATE IS A BUD...
Here is my smile that floats leaving a trail
of laughs...

HERE ARE MY WINGS THAT BEAT...
In ice & in heat?
YEAH!
YES!
The Universe creating a face
peeping from a cushioned cave
in fleeing guises of meat...
ETERNALLY...   FOREVER...

This book has been printed in handset Joanna and Tuscan Graile types by letterpress in two editions: a) 1200 copies bound in paper; and b) 50 copies on handmade paper, bound in boards and signed by the author.